52 Questions and Answers for Singles:

Ask the Right QUESTION, Get the Right LIFE!

Fred L. Hodge
&
Linda G. Hodge

Copyright 2016 by Fred L. Hodge and Linda G. Hodge

All rights reserved. In accordance with the U.S. Copyright Act of 1976, the scanning, uploading, and electronic sharing of any part of this book without the permission of the publisher is unlawful piracy and theft of the author's intellectual property. If you would like to use material from this book, (other than review purposes) prior written permission must be obtained by contacting the publisher at info at knowledgepowerbooks.com.

Thank you for your support of the author's rights.

ISBN: 978-099766223-8
Library of Congress Control Number: 2016943587
Edited by: Penny Scott
Cover Design: Juan Roberts, Creative Lunacy, Inc.

Published by
Knowledge Power Books
Valencia, California 91355
www.knowledgepowerbooks.com

Printed in the United States of America

Introduction

This book is all about "empowerment." Consequently, you aren't able to make a quality decision based on knowledge that you haven't acquired. Knowledge is the fuel that qualifies you to make a calculated decision about your life: the career you chose, the lifestyle you feel you desire, the relationships you allow to nurture, develop, and ultimately choose as your mate.

Unfortunately, there are countless relationships that didn't have the fuel to keep it moving in the right direction. They were built on cheap imitations of unrealistic expectations, faulted-thinking, wrong perceptions and unforeseen danger signals. Viewing a relationship through faulted lens will undeniably cause a "crash."

Therefore, prior to you considering a relationship, you must examine your own lens. What exactly are you seeing, and from what perspective are you viewing it in respect to a wholesome relationship? If you are desperate, then everyone that appears to be a possible prospect looks to be a likely candidate for marriage. Coincidently, if there isn't anyone on the planet that meets your qualifications, you may possibly be unrealistic in your expectations. Here's a typical example. Val has always imagined the perfect relationship: despite growing up in a single-parent home, and acquiring the job as a live-in sitter for her smaller siblings. As a teen, it was an arduous job her mother gave her freely without her consent.

Val vowed to herself during those years that her future life will be per-fect. Daydreaming had become an imaginary game, bringing temporary relief from a life of continual work and chores. She would create images in her mind of her "Prince Charming," who came riding in her neigh-borhood on a white horse. By magic, he gently spooked her up from the ground. Oh, how she despised the responsibilities that weighed her down. It felt similar to wearing an invisible life-jacket.

So, moving forward her aspirations in life was one of rescue. Therefore, her expectation list was "over the top" and somewhat unrealistic to say the least. A practical and balanced approach must be incorporated in choosing a mate for life. No one comes into your life to make it perfect: instead, he/she comes to complement and enhance your life.

Ralph on the other hand, was a "mama's boy" in every sense of the word. Being raised from a single mom who carried the guilt of her son not having a man's presence in the house was not what she bargained for in his life. Miss Alice, his mother, had done the best she could dealing with the deck of cards she was handed. Despite, her diligence she had failed at equipping him for his journey in life. A mother's love is enormous, but can also be hindering, if not applied properly. Without the proper tools in developing a young boy into manhood, results can be devastating for the woman that is the recipient of his lack of maturity, discipline and self-control. So, we know how the story ends. Ralph hadn't a clue of what it means to be a "real" man and was always looking for handouts from women. Besides, his mother had taught him well!

In the following pages there will be questions and answers that assist in your approach of successfully determining Mr. & Mrs. Right. The hard questions must be addressed and explored in considering a mate. When you know where you want to go, a map must be designed to reach the destination. This book serves as your map for reaching your destination, safe and sound. Fortunately, there is always a criterion that must be mea-sured prior to entering a possible relationship. Human nature has a tendency to gravitate toward what "looks" good despite what is necessarily advantageous for them. There is a multitude of unseen realities that is either ignored or justified by our need of attachments.

Possibly, you have ignored what you are "seeing" and what you are "hearing," because your emotional need is greater than the truth that you are experiencing. Consequently, this may be the reason you settled for less than you desired.

These questions and answers are designed to heighten your vigilant introspection of sound judgment. So, what can you expect from reading this book. You can expect to have a pivotal change in your life as you navigate through these pages. Therefore, you will become more aware of the pitfalls hindering your thought process, and the choices you have made in your past. And, finally, self-awareness will begin to immerse from the depth of your soul. Buckle up, and enjoy your ride to a safe, secure landing!

Question 1

While dating, when should you start talking about personal things such as family, kids, credit score and sex?

Fred L. Hodge: (FH)

Dating was created for you to get to know each other. This is why you don't do anything intimate during this stage. You shouldn't even kiss: kissing and other forms of affection starts tying your souls together. The intimacy will get you locked in and you don't even know the person yet. Dating is for discovery: you don't need to have intimate conversations until both of you decide that you want to court each other with progression toward marriage.

You become ready for the courting stage when you believe that the relationship needs to be explored in a deeper level, and you know everything has been placed on the table. You are saying to each other, "We're going to be exclusive to each other, and now we are going to start talking serious talk."

When you move to this stage of courtship you ask, "Can we be husband and wife?" You need to discuss these issues because what if you want to have 5 children and your companions says, "Oh no! I don't want to have any babies." Then, that's a no-brainer. It should be a deal breaker. Say, "Thanks for being my friend," and move on.

Walk away because you will end up fighting during your marriage. Why experience all of that warfare when you can just as easily choose somebody else? Stop being desperate! You think this is the only person in the world, that you have to accept whatever comes, no. It's OK to hold out if they don't meet the particular expectation that you have. If you settle, against your better judgment, you are not going to be with them too much longer. You're going to be too miserable and you don't need misery in your life.

Linda G. Hodge: (LH)

Before you get into the more personal topics, you can start talking about your values. Whatever your values are, that's what's going to govern your life. What do you value? What is really important to you in life? What is a deal breaker for you in a relationship? What is your family like? How did you grow up? These are good things to talk about because it lets you know the challenges that this person may possibly be dealing with in their lives.

As you begin to dig and ask questions you've determined the possibility of what could be underlying in that person. So, you ask questions about what their values are, and what their experiences in life have been. Find out how their experiences have shaped them to be what they are today. You also have to know what you've learned from the experiences that you've had. What does your "never again" list look like? Ask questions like these before you start talking about intimacy issues. Ladies, can I get permission to get a little below the belt? Thank you, for saying, "Yes." You don't need to know the size of his hands and feet, or how he likes it and when does he like it, morn-ing or night? Questions like, "How many times a week do you want it?"

should be off limits in the dating stage. We want to jump all into those questions because many times that's where we live: we live in the flesh and so we want to go there. Stop yourself and say, "No, let's deal with the real issues at hand." Find out what makes them tick besides sex.

Who are they? Who are you? When you go home and take off the make-up, the weave, the body shaper, who are you? Who are you really?

When all of your defenses are down; when you are not trying to impress, that's who I want to know about. All of this other stuff, this "cute stuff " is not going to matter at midnight. I need to know who I am going to wake up to in the morning. I need to know what type of attitude I'm going to face when you awake. I need to know your temperament. Now, that should give you a perspective from both a man and a woman.

Question 2

What is the proper way to date in the church?

FH:

First of all, you have to be careful when dating. When you put the chemistry of a man and a woman together, it automatically progresses because that is God's intentions. So, you must gain a new perspective on dating, and understand the importance of establishing a friendship. You have to ask yourself, "Can I be friends even if I don't get married?" Let's say you are dating a young man at the church and you guys are good friends, then the dating ends and he marries someone else. Are you going to be resentful? Are you going to show a hateful attitude? Did you let yourself pretend and fantasize about something that was never established? You cannot presume that people who want to be your friend also want to be your mate.

The perspective must be clear: this is just a friend of mine and you can't play into it or read more into it. Don't be imbalanced in your thinking just because he spoke to you: suddenly you see yourself with 10 babies and 3 houses. You cannot allow yourself to go through that. You have to establish boundaries and parameters. So, make dating a very safe environment. Don't do the house-to-house thing: stay away from each other's houses.

When you date, you should meet at the allocated place. Make a plan and stick to it. "We're going to dinner at *Claim Jumpers*™. I'll meet you there at 6." Or, "I'll pick you up from church, we'll leave your car there, we can ride together, and when it's over, I'll drop you back at church." Just as soon as you take her home to her apartment, you are in an intimate place. You're in a place of warfare now, and you have to decide whether you're going to go inside or not. You start looking at each other with lonely eyes, all of a sudden, he's too tired to drive home. He says, "I don't want to get in a wreck." "Oh, I have a couch come on up." And, you get yourselves in trouble.

Dating cannot become intimate. Information such as, what you make on your check, is none of their business. You guys are just friends hanging out. You are not planning a future together at this stage. That is how you have to treat it: if you don't treat it that way then you can create soul ties. And, become very hurt when it doesn't work out. Or, someone better comes along, and you drop that person leaving him/her heartbro-ken. So that's why you stay away from intimacy, you keep them at a friendship level.

LH:

You just have to create your bound-aries and establish how you are go-ing to do it. If you are private and don't want people in your business, then don't tell people. If you don't want people to know that you're dating somebody, don't tell them.

FH:

Here is the problem: we have this secular idea of dating. Oftentimes, it means you are my boyfriend or you're my girlfriend: I have now taken possession of you. Worldly dating says, "You owe me now because you are mine."

That is where we have to eradicate intimacy. You don't belong to each other. You can't claim anyone unless you are in the courting stage preparing for marriage. You just have to ask them, "Why do you want to date me?" If they say, "Well, I just want to be friends," then you have to negotiate whether or not you want that type of relationship. Ask and find out if they are dating you for discovery to see if you are compatible for some kind of future. That's what you need to know because you could be wasting a whole lot of your time on someone who is trying to get over on you. So you really have to sit down and talk in this dating process.

Other than that, you can hang out with a group. Go to the movies together, and from time to time, have lunch or dinner together. But, we are not going to begin to enmesh ourselves in some kind of intimate trap to where we've taken possession of each other without vows and commitment.

Another thing, stop sharing inti-mate things with the person you are dating. They should not know everything about you on the first date. If you don't want to get into the trap of intimacy don't share personal information. Don't talk about "Oh, I just love it when a man breathes down my neck." Don't do all of that! Do that, and the next thing you know, he's going to be breathing down your neck. <u>Remember</u>, you are just friends.

Question 3

I know the Bible says to wait till marriage to have sex. But, how do we know it's going to be any good?

FH:

Sounds like a soul tie is involved. Somebody hooked you up, and now you are going to end up having comparisons. In other words, it leaves you open to compare when you get married wondering will they be as good as the souls ties you've been with.

LH:

You have to realize that you can make anything good. You can *absolutely* make anything good: you don't have to try it out first to see if it's worthy. Also, it's understandable that many of you have that urge to "try it out first." But just because it is good one time, doesn't mean it is <u>always</u> going to be good. So, that's another element that you want to consider as well. But, when you are married, you can make it all good, sweetie! You can make anything good.

FH:

You don't have to "try on the shoe" to make sure it fits. What you can do, when it's time is you can attend seminars. We have a variety of books in our library: *Intended for Pleasure: Sex Technique and Sexual Fulfillment in Christian Marriage* is one of those books. It's written by Ed Wheat and Gaye Wheat, a Christian psychologist and sex relationship expert. This book helps you understand the male and female body, and how to do things correctly. So, don't use the excuse that you need to experiment before the marriage.

LH:

You both have the basic foundation to make it enjoyable. There isn't a whole lot that you have to do to manipulate that, right? Although there are different sizes and different shapes, you can make it good when you are married. How you arouse your spouse or how you perform your foreplay may determine your orgasm. Right before you get married you may want to discuss a few things with your fiancé or get a couple sex books and talk about some things with each other.

But you don't need to experiment to see what does and doesn't work. When you're married you can always make a little adjustment here and a little adjustment there to make it better. If you find out it isn't big enough for you, then have him take an erection pill or Viagra to help a brother out and you are good to go. You've got the whole night laid out so you are good to go.

Question 4

How do you know when it's time to date again, or just rebounding after a break-up?

LH:

You should never rebound, it's not healthy. A rebound is saying, "I'm going to get somebody because I'm hurt!" That's the definition of a rebound. You are using this new person as a substitute for what has happened to you in a previous relationship. You are supposed to move on to a new relationship when you're healed and you're ready to move forward.

FH:

You have to delete the baggage that came with that old relationship! First, you must become healed. You don't want to transfer the old hurts and pain you experienced from your previous relationship into your new one. Like Pastor Linda said, don't try to substitute the new relationship as a healing from the old. You can't properly recover by exchanging one person with another in your life.

You can only recover by both you and God taking care of the hurt that has been perpetrated on your life and heart. You need to be whole, and have a healed outlook on your life. You may have some questions when someone rejects you or when something goes wrong and you start questioning your self-esteem. What happened to me? Was I not good enough? Why did they do this to me? You've got to answer those questions and return to a place of courage. If you don't, you are going to dump all of the trash that you picked up in that old relationship. And, you are going to make them feel miserable. When you aren't healed, you replicate on people what you are feeling about yourself.

My wife is an awesome person because she helped me the first year we got married. I used to talk about my ex all of the time because I was so hurt by it. She would just let me vent, but really that was not the proper way. The proper way would have been for me to already have been healed. I don't know if we jumped the gun by getting married in a month or if it was those around us wanting us to get married: so they could stop helping me with my four kids. However, knowing each other for a month and jumping into a relationship where all of our baggage begins to spill out was not healthy. I should have been healed from of the memory of my ex. I needed to be healed from having a certain attitude whenever I thought about my ex, rather than spewing it out on my wife. And, relate to her and life from a place of hurt. So, that is why God had to come in and straighten me out. I mean he had to threaten me. God actually threatened me.

One day I was in the car riding by myself and He said, "Son, you are about to lose one of the best things that I could have ever given you." I said, "What are you talking about?" He said, "I'm tired of you treating my daughter the way you are acting. You are going to have to stop." Once I heard from Him, I ran home. I repented to her, cried in her arms, and I told her that I would never let the devil do this again. From that part we became partners, and from there we started to move forward. All of the talk about the old relationship deceased. I asked the Holy Spirit to help me. I told her to be patient with me, but that stuff just went to the grave. I started concentrating on her and our relationship.

Question 5

Is it a sin and will I go to Hell for looking at pornography and fantasizing, while masturbating?

LH:

The Bible says in Philippians 4:8, "Finally, brothers and sisters, whatever is true, whatever is noble, whatever is right, whatever is pure, whatever is lovely, whatever is admirable – if anything is excellent or praiseworthy think about such things." Imagination is a powerful tool, and it's our responsibility to monitor what goes in our mind. You have to be careful what you practice because what happens is it can turn into addictions. All of a sudden, what you used to do every other week, you are doing every week. Then, you want more of it and it escalates to 3 times a week, and then you find yourself doing it every day. You have to be very careful with opening those types of doors because what may seem simple or harmless can become an addiction: Before you know it, that addiction can become a monster with an insatiable appetite.

The Bible also tells us in 2 Corinthians 10:5, "Casting down imaginations, and every high thing that exalteth itself against the knowledge of God, and bringing into captivity every thought to the obedience of Christ." It is our responsibility, to dismantle every thought that is contrary to the Word to be demonic. Images grow and yield fruit. We must ask the question, "What is growing in our mental gardens?"

Question 6

You said that in the spirit realm, there is not male or female. What is the spirit realm and where is it?

FH:

Spirit realm is the unseen realm that is a whole Bible teaching within itself. When God created Adam and Eve, He scooped up some clay, formed it into a male body, and blew into his nostrils the breath of life. That what he blew into him was spirit. The scripture says after God blew into him he became a living soul. So the mind that God had given him came alive, and it had personality after the spirit and entered into your vessel. It is a huge teaching and I would need more time to teach on that.

Question 7

What is sex for, for us to even have a sex drive?

FH:

God made us to procreate. In the beginning when he made Adam and Eve, He told them "Now be fruitful, multiply, and replenish the earth." So, it was by the purpose of God that He put a sex drive in humanity to cause them to continually bring forth seed. Seed or children are the inheritance of the Lord to bring forth His purposes during their generation. God has to perpetuate every generation. That's why He's given human kind a sex drive because without it there would be no more children. That's not all that is for. He does give it to you for fun: also for relief of pressure and tension in your body. But y'all go to the gym. That'll work just as good. It won't feel as good, but it'll work just the same.

Question 8

God wants us to have passion for Him. Can you explain what passion is? How is passion created? How does it go away?

FH:

Wow! These are some hard questions. The scripture says whatever you hunger and thirst for, that's what you are going to receive. The level of your hunger and thirst is the level that you will be filled. So now, what is hunger and thirst? Those are appetites. When your body becomes hungry, there is a force in you which drives you to eat. When you are thirsty, there is a force within you, which drives you to drink. So thereby, you have this passion, and this power that is a force that drives you to fulfill a need. The same with sexual appetite: there is a desire in you: a force, that drives you until you get that need met. So, we must turn that force and passion towards God. Now, start having a hunger for God. Turn that craving toward God. Turn that desire toward God.

Question 9

If it is not a sin for us to have a sex drive, what is lusting?

FH:

In James, it says, "Let no man say when he is tempted, I am tempted of God, for God cannot be tempted with evil, neither does he tempt any man. But every man is tempted when he is drawn away of his own lusts, and enticed. Then when lust has conceived it brings forth sin and sin when it is finished brings forth death." What does it mean to conceive? Think of being pregnant: it means when that sperm and egg come together. So it is not until a thing actually becomes tangible in your heart that you have now entered into lust. The temptation is not lust. When the picture comes, that's not lust. When you watched it on TV that is not lust you experienced. The lust entered when you began to fantasize about what you watched until it created a desire to have it. Now you are in lust.

What we are saying is that you have to manage your sex drive. You can't allow it to get to the place where you have fed it so many images now the appetite is saying, "I'm hungry, feed me! Feed me, Feed me now!" You can't afford to fellowship with things that are going to bring you to that place of compulsion. You have to manage your sex drive, and try to keep it from getting to the point of arousal. Just because you have one doesn't mean you are in sin. But, it's when you allow yourself to get into a world of fantasy and conceive a desire to the degree, where you are going to work it out in a tangible or intangible way. You have just entered into a place of lust.

LH:

I do know that for people who have various addictions, there are 12-Step Programs and organizations available, if you need help with that. There are countless people whose addictions have gotten out of hand, and are in need of extra help. If you are struggling, not only do you need to apply the word of God and keep coming to church, but you also need to continue doing everything you know to do that is right. Coupled with some outside help, that can minister to that part of you in order to prevent a detachment from taking place.

So, you just have to be very careful because what you feed is what will grow. If you already know you have a high sex drive, and you don't curtail your appetite, all you are doing is adding fuel to the fire. So, you have to learn how to cast those imaginations down and divert those images and mindsets to something else. Otherwise, it will grow and continue to grow, and before you know it, you solicit somebody off the street to fulfill a need. You have to be careful of your thoughts. Monitor it and gain the victory.

FH:

You have to know yourself. You know when you are letting yourself go too far: you know. But the problem is that you don't want to stop yourself because it feels good. You are pacifying a need. You have to know yourself enough, not to let yourself go there. You got to reprimand yourself. "Stop it!" Let's try it, say out loud, "Stop it!" You really have to tell yourself to stop. Because you are the only one who can master your will, you have to have self control.

LH:

There was a gentleman that we knew that made a powerful statement: I still remember it. He was caught up on drugs and was delivered. He said that he doesn't even drink coffee because his former addiction was so strong. He was setting precautions for himself in order not to create another addiction. Sometimes, you have to be extremely tight on yourself: to the point that you pull back (from over eating, eating chocolate, looking at TV, etc.). Oftentimes, people will do anything to substitute their addiction. So, they may eat to substitute having sex. Or, they may smoke instead of dealing with anxiety. You must learn how to deal with your issues: you can't put a band aid on them, and think everything will continue to be OK. Otherwise, you are going to live in bondage for the rest of your life.

Question 10

What if you have a soul tie with someone (that you believe God sent in your life) who is God-fearing, BUT who has different beliefs, concerning Jesus being the son of God?

FH:

You're messing with your salvation. You are entertaining a lot of trouble, and lots of warfare. Are you ready for that? There is the possibility of having a lot of disagreements. What create difficulties in relationships are communication, sex, money, and religion. Most don't play with their beliefs: you think you can get them with your "good loving." However, once you get married, they are going to want to raise those children as Muslim, or Catholics, or Buddhists: whatever religion they were raised as children. Are you prepared to do warfare your entire life over trying to rear your children in Christ?

LH:

People don't play with their beliefs. Many times, your faith is in your core value. And you don't go in and out, changing people's core values when that core value is established. It is hard to change. It's almost impossible, unless God does it: it is impossible for you to change it. If you think you are going to change it, you are in deception. Instead of getting yourself all wrapped up in that warfare, loose yourself. You will never be on the same page, and there will always be potential for war in your house because of it. We have talked to people 30-40 years in that are dealing with it, and I've never seen them change. Don't do it just because you want a man or a woman. Desperation will cost you every time.

I know people who are seriously in regret and wondering why they made that decision. One woman I know of married a Muslim, and thought he was going to come to Christianity. That guy is giving her so much trouble and heartache she has gotten sick in her body: many times, from working with all of that stress in dealing with him. It was all a deception. If you want a Christian guy, then you marry one. Don't go into any relationship thinking that you are going to change that person.

Question 11

How did you know Pastor Linda was "The one" that God had for your life? How and when did you know?

FH:

He told me. I mean I was hurting, so I was not open to choosing at the time. I was just going to work, taking care of my kids and I had started the church. Those things were my passion and that's where my heart was focused. I went home to live with my parents so that I would keep myself out of any danger. I didn't want some woman floating in my life or in my children's lives, causing havoc. So, I was under submission to my mother and father. I mean, I was a grown man, but I did what was right to keep me right.

So, I brought myself under submission. After a year or so, my family started praying for me to have a wife. That scared me. I said "Oh God, I'm not going to let people give me a wife." So, I start telling Him what I wanted in a wife, I made a list. Someone wanted to know how detailed should that list be: it should be extremely detailed because you are going to get what you desire. Thus, if you desire it, make sure you put it on that list. As time passed, the Lord brought her to me, and told me it was her, "this is your wife."

It was hard because I had been so hurt and messed up. I had to ask God to freeze my nature, or I wouldn't have made it. You have to understand that after nine years of being married and having sex, then suddenly you aren't married anymore, you have to curtail your appetite. One day, I was crying and praying to God and told him this is it. I told him, "If you don't help me tonight, I'm going out to find a prostitute or someone who is willing. I need you to help me." That night the Lord came in, He wrapped me in his arms, and I was alright. I woke up the next day and the desire was gone and for that year I didn't pursue or crave sexual interaction.

LH:

You didn't even masturbate?

FH:

No, I'm telling you God will do it for you. When I met Pastor Linda, my nature was shut down. Once we agreed that we were going to obey God; I hugged her and I stood at attention, you know what that means? My desire came back and that's why we got married within a month. Because that desire was so strong and we wanted to do right because of our love for God and the position we were in, we got married quickly. I was pastoring a church and didn't want to fall. So, we got married in one month. That was over 34 years ago, and now we are growing old together.

Question 12

What about a homosexual soul tie?

FH:

Understand this: your flesh will form an addiction to whatever you make available to it. And, whatever you expose it to.

LH:

Also, the flesh if you allow it to go there, will think that unlawful, or sinful appetites are good.

FH:

So the Bible says there is no good thing in the flesh. It cannot be trusted. You have to constrain it. You've got to control it, or it will get you in trouble. Your body is the vessel that God gave you to travel around the earth. It has appetites in it.

Question 13

Why does it seem exciting to sneak around?

LH:

That is what happens in an adulterous relationship: some people experience excitement while sneaking around. But, if you have to sneak and hide in the car all of the time, does it really feel exciting? While we're out walking, we've witnessed numerous "couples," driving two separate cars up to the mountain. Then, say their goodbyes with kisses and other forms of affection before going separate ways.

FH:

And see, that is all part of the satanic ploy! It makes it more mysterious, and even more satisfying to the soul that you are receiving something that you are not supposed to possess. Don't trust your flesh! I am a born-again, spirit-filled preacher, and I don't trust my flesh. I won't let myself get close like that. If I think we've looked at each other too long, I'm out. I won't see a woman by myself. You can call it what you want, but I won't give it a chance.

Question 14

Is perversion really wrong?

LH:

It's the wrong thinking pattern! Some people have immersed themselves in so much perversion that they receive orgasms off pain. It's like they enjoy pain. Many have become so out-of-control their spirit has caused them to hang themselves. They claim a certain orgasm is created through that pain. And, others have gone too far, accidentally killing themselves.

FH:

Because of perversion, people have even formed an addiction to being beaten: they enjoy being whipped and like alternative piercings. Then, several report not having enough and wanting to be pierced everywhere. So, you can form an addiction from perverse ideas.

LH:

I was listening to Les Brown on the radio and he had people come on the air and talk about their various relationships. One woman said that she was in a wonderful relationship for 15 years, but it was actually with another woman. She said they were just friends at first, attended excursions together, and dined out together. All of a sudden, because she spent so much time with her, she began to fantasize about having a relationship with the other woman. She said that she'd never been in a homosexual relationship. However, she surprisingly began to be attracted to that person. One of the times they were spending time together, they took it to another level. They've been together over 15 years now. While over-spending time with someone so much, she allowed the spirit of perversion to enter and completely alter a friendship.

FH:

But, it is an unnatural affection: that's what the Bible calls it. That's why you don't trust your flesh. That's why we have guidelines in the Bible that tells us to set the perimeter you live in your flesh: because flesh is nothing but soil. You can sow anything in it and you can grow any crop.

Question 15

How can women not attract unwanted physical attention? What is the proper attire for a woman of God?

FH:

Oooh, let me talk. It is my perspective that a woman should not try to hide who she is because of some perverted mentality of man. However, it is also my opinion that a woman ought not to pervert herself to get the attention of a man. I love my wife's figure, and for a long time my wife would not show it off. We would have talks about it because she would always wear droopy clothes. I had to tell her, "You are too gorgeous for this: you are not a grandma. Well, you are a grandma, but you are not a granny!" I had to explain to her that I appreciate who God made you, and that is who I want to see. I want to see who God made you. So she started wearing fashionable clothes that showed her silhouette.

A woman is a woman, and you are not going to hide that. Just because you don't want anyone to look at you that way, well that is on them. Now, when you got them all hugged up and hanging out to where we can see everything, then that is a problem. God gave you that, and He wasn't trying to hide it. I think there is a way to moderately dress, where you can show your figure without any perverted intention. I want grandmothers to be grandmothers, but also the ladies to be ladies. Men, you dress like men should, and women, dress how women should. You should embrace who you are, because that is how God made you.

Question 16

Can sex just be sex? Is it possible to not have an emotional attachment with someone you don't have feelings for?

FH:

Yes sex can be purely physical. But, if it is on a consistent basis, you will start forming an attachment. To prove my point, when you went to college and you used to get drunk and have sex with someone, you didn't form an attachment. You didn't even know the person's name: you just had a good time. Afterwards, you went back to studying and there was no soul tie attached. So, sex can just be sex. But, if you continually have sex with that same person, that's indicative that something has made an attachment in your soul arena. For the mere fact that you keep returning: Something keeps you going back. So, it's not just sex anymore. Now, you have tied together.

LH:

It's really an emotional attachment as well because you keep going back. You are allowing your body to be used: outside of the perimeter of God's creation. 1 Corinthians 6:19-20 states, "Do you know that your bodies are temples of the Holy Spirit, who is in you, whom you have received from God? You are not your own; you were brought at a price. Therefore, honor God with your bodies."

FH:

Women need to be very careful because this is how God created you: to be an emotional person. In His creativity, to differentiate between the female and the male, God gave you that ability to bring expression and creativity into a relationship. Thus, your emotions are more vulnerable than a man. He is thinking rationally, considering the reasonable thought process. You're thinking more about feelings and emotions, and when you are driven by emotions, you tend to form more of an attachment. He is thinking, "I need to satisfy my sexual drive. I need to get my needs met." You're considering, "I want somebody to love me. I want somebody to embrace me. I want to feel accepted." And, you're willing to give your body as a price to feel those things in your life.

LH:

Do men have emotional attachments?

FH:

Yes, they do, but it isn't as apparent as women. Eventually, he will get into an emotional tie. But at the onset, his mind is all about conquering the prey. That is all he is doing, getting his need met.

Question 17

People say sex is such an emotional thing for women, hereas, men can have sex with no emotional attachment. What if you're a woman who can be intimate without an attachment? Or, is a woman attached without knowing she is? Earlier you said, "Once a man conquers something he moves on." What about once a woman conquers something she moves on? Why are there so many double standards in our society?

FH:

It's not a double standard. It's simply the way you've been created. It's just a different chemical makeup. Men are typically made by reasoning: they work by ego. Women usually work by feelings and emotions. You are more relational: a man is more competitive – that is his nature. He has been created that way in order to seek employment and make a living. He can get out there and fight for his family. He's going to bring the bread home. You are the one that wants to know all of the questions about his day. You ask a series of questions. "How was your day honey? What did you do when you went to work? Who did you have coffee with during your break? Did you make the deal?" She wants to relate because she wants to feel emotionally connected. It's just the two different ways that we've been created.

Now, some women can embody those traits to where they are going along, conquering and have a little black book with all kinds of names listed.

LH:

So, you are saying that women do it as well? They will take from men just to get their needs met. It happens both ways?

FH:

Yes, it happens to both. But, it is a paradigm shift and against the original creation. Oftentimes, women will take on that stance because she's gotten deeply hurt. She thinks, "Well, I am going to use them or get me some money so she'll start conquering men in that fashion."

Question 18

How do you get control of your will?

FH:

This is an awesome question because the will is the key. We understand that we are going to prosper even as our soul prospers. We have to understand the components of the Soul, and that is my mind, intellect, imagination, emotion, and my will. So, in order for me to really get control of my life, I have to understand those components. And, how they function and then how I have mastery through these 5 components. Now, how do I get control of my will, which is specifically one component which is the enforcer of decisions that I make. You deduce with your mind and then you make the decision and carry it out with your will. Your will makes your body perform. Thus, your will is very important. We look at Jesus, when it comes to looking at the will. Jesus was in the Garden of Gethsemane experiencing terrible, agonizing painful deductions: "If I do this, I'll be separated from the Father. My flesh will be torn apart. I don't know if I can do this." So, He tells the Father, "If there is any other way, remove this cup from me and find another way." And then, He prays and He comes up with this answer. In Luke 22:42 it says, "Father, if you are willing, take this cup from me; yet not my will, but yours be done." There has to be something going on in His thought process for him now to establish a new course and set his will to endure this traumatic situation that was set before him.

And, what we found out in Hebrews 12:2, "For the joy set before Him he endured the cross, scorning its shame, and sat down at the right hand of the throne of God." Here, it talks about some of his mediations, and what he actually experienced. For the joy that was set before him, he endured the cross. During the time, he was saying remove the cup. And the next moment he is saying, "Ok, not my will, but your will be done." We know a change took place. He reassigned some thoughts. He gave new meaning to the cross in order to set his will. You and I are made to function like this, we move away from pain and toward pleasure. But, we have the ability to define the difference between pain and pleasure. We have that ability to create definitions, and we have to be very careful to take our definitions from the word of God. The enemy can get in there, manipulate our mind, and make things seem painful, which are actually good. Then, try to convince us to believe pleasurable things are actually bad for us. So, what Jesus did is He reassigned the meaning. If I go to the cross, I will make my Father happy. I will please Him: I will extract millions of souls from darkness to the light. Billions will reach heaven because of my one sacrifice. Essentially, God gave it new meaning. I'm going to look beyond the cross to see the joy that's set before me. So now, I can set my will knowing how I'm created. I am made to move away from pain and toward pleasure. So, I can endure this painful situation for a moment: and endure pleasurable situations forever more. Such as, if I have sex with this guy what is the long-term outcome? Well, I am going to feel shame afterward, and feel condemned because I violated the Lord's law. He possibly is going to share the experience with his friends and talk to them. If it's a guy in church, he may now tell his buddies in church, "I did this with her and vice versa." Women talk about guys, too. Guys don't feel left out. They talk about you, too. But, you have all of these components in place. You have to say, "Do I have pleasure for a moment? Or, do I resist this moment for the long-term affects and hold out for my husband?" And then, you give it new meaning, where you can set your will to say, "No, I'm sorry that's too painful." Your 5 minutes or your 5 seconds, however long you last, that determines your level of pleasure. That's a whole big teaching lesson. But, I gave you enough information. Now, you can deal with choices that you have to make because the chemistry is that we move away from pain to protection. That's why God gave us these types of sensory components. You put your hands in fire and it burns you. You say, "Never again, will I put my hand in fire again." Why? PAIN! That's how you're built: to protect yourself. Now, you can define these situations as either painful or pleasurable by the deductions that you go through in our mind.

Question 19

When praying for a wife how specific should you be?

FH:

VERY! Very Specific because what was that old song? Y'all forgive me, "Short Ones, Round Ones, Big ones too." Remember the song? Right! Was that too far back in my day? It was talking about the variety of a woman is so extensive, and it's according to a man's taste. You want to pray for what you need in life. Some men are very attracted to larger frame women, and small women are not appealing to them. They want her to have meat on her bones. Other men prefer skinny women, and they want her to stay skinny even after she has a delivered a child. You can't defraud people, and you can't marry them and not tell them your expectations because some expectations are not justifiable. When a woman has a baby, her body has been made to produce. Therefore, she is going to gain weight and there's going to be changes in her chemistry. A brother better be informed and have a good understanding that it's going to happen. Because then he becomes abusive after she brings forth a child, and he has his mind set that she is supposed to maintain a certain figure. There are more things to talk about during the time you are dating.

LH:

Also, when a man is choosing a woman, what we have seen many times is that they are choosing them based on exterior beauty. They are not looking on the inside of that woman. And, that is something that they really have to live with. Beauty is fleeting. One day you may have 36x24x36. But, in another 5 years down the line, like Pastor said after you had a baby, you may be 46x56x60. So, you can't go by that because people change from one day to the next. You can't pick a woman based off her looks. But, what you can do is pick a woman based on her values.

FH:

We are talking about being very specific. My specificity was that I needed a partner in life. The beauty thing was not at the top of my list. I asked God to give me someone that loved Him just as much as I did. Or more, because I knew there was safety in that. Say safety, "Safety." Unless this partner of mine is connected to God, I'm always going to have trouble. So, my first request was she has to love you as much as me. So, no matter what trouble we have in life, I know we are going to make it because we both serve the same God. And, we both love him and that means we're both going to do His will in the end. We may be angry at each other for a minute, but I know that both of us will choose God over either of us. He's the one that's going to ultimately keep us together. That was the number one thing on my list. And then, I asked God that she would enjoy working in ministry with me, and that she would work along side of me and easy on the eyes.

Question 20

Who can I talk to when I feel anxious about marriage and I start rushing things?

LH:

You have to talk to someone who is going to give you an accurate look at your state of well-being. You can't talk to girlfriends who are in your current situation.

FH:

Who is as hungry as you?

LH:

You have to talk to someone who will make it very clear and plain.

FH:

Who will bring you back to reality?

LH:

If your girlfriend can't do it, then you need to seek a higher counsel, connect with a mentor in your life or someone who has wisdom. And, who can bring balance and proper thinking.

Question 21

How do you get rid of anger from a violation experienced through a predator? How can you move on from being raped by a family member? How can you forgive or move on from that rape?

LH:

First of all, Satan loves to regurgitate the memory of what you experienced over and over again to incarcerate you. He wants to paralyze your ability to live life to its fullest. So what you must do is understand the scriptures. We think that forgiving is releasing them from the responsibility of what they've done. Forgiveness doesn't release a person from responsibility. The Lord put into the scripture that when you repent there are some sins which you must bear fruit of.

Point in case, repentance in the case of a family rape or child molestation: that person actually needs to go to jail. Even if you forgive them, you should report them and they should do time. That's the fruits of repentance that people must understand. Here are the consequences I suffered for the bad decisions that I've made when I violated another human being. And, in order to train my flesh and eradicate this from my soul, I have to endure the consequences of my actions.

Many people get stuck from not forgiving because they feel if I forgive them, then they are released from the consequences of their sin against me. There are sins unto death, and the Lord says, "I do not say that you should pray for those."

But there are sins not unto death, where you can pray for a person and actually get forgiveness for that person even though they are not seeking forgiveness. So there are certain sins that cause certain consequences that must be paid. The whole rule is, "God is not mocked what a man sows that shall he also reap."

We can do things in action, get forgiveness, and still have to endure the consequences or fruit of that action. So that is why we have to be careful in our choices. You can choose to lay down knowing that God's grace will cover you when you get up. But, when the seed is planted, you will be pregnant. And, He is not going to abort the baby to cover you.

Now, back to the perpetrator, the forgiveness aspect is not just for them it's for you. Whatever sin you retain, that sin you entertain and now it incarcerates you. If you keep the offense inside of you, it is working emotional death. It stays inside of you, and it begins to mold your character, and starts to change or alter your true personality. Have you ever seen a basket case who's endured traumatic situations? It changes them entirely because they dwell on it, and it drives their soul crazy. Their character is totally changed because they entertained, meditated, and held onto the offense and the sin itself that the perpetrator committed has now becomes theirs.

That is why the Lord said, "Let it go," because you are not capable of holding that in your soul without it violating you more, and then paralyzing your future.

So, the way to get past the event is to forgive and release. And, notice what I said up front, you are not releasing them from the act. You're releasing them from the violation against you, so that it will not stay in you. And, once you let that go, you have to walk in faith for the forgiveness. So, when your mind brings it back and ask, "Are you seriously going to forgive them?" You say, "I've let that go, I've cast that care unto the Lord and I'm pursing my life." You have to fight the good fight of faith.

Question 22

If you have been sexually violated and think sex is bad, how do you reverse your mind to think that sex is good? How do you release your mind of the sexual violation?

FH:

That kind of goes with what I just said about one way to reverse your outlook or perspective of it is to understand that sex was not created by man. Instead, it was created for man by God. God did not create anything nasty and bad: it is how man manages it that it transforms the experience into nasty and bad. So, you must begin to look at it from God's perspective. God did this to bring glory to Himself. He made sexuality for humanity's procreation, and in order to show intimacy, oneness, and duplicate His relationship with us with another person. Every time a couple comes together, it is worship unto God. Otherwise, I am violating my body with someone outside the rule that God set. Consequently, I am violating the temple of my God – from the original intent of its purpose.

Question 23

How do you know if he is the one?

FH:

Well, I would look at a few things. First, I would look at his spiritual lifestyle. I would consider if he is filled with the spirit, saved, and born again. Is he a man of faith? Ladies and gentlemen, you do not want to marry an unbeliever. One of the true prerequisites: is if a man loves his mother, and I'm not saying a momma's boy, that's two different things. Also, you must ask yourself, "Does he or she fit with my destiny?" Will he/she be competent with me, complete me, or bring division in my life? What are his/her core values in life?

LH:

Chemistry is not always a good judge of character. It is sometimes referred to what we call, "love at first sight." It sees what it wants to see. But once the other side is revealed, those wonderful characteristics vanish like the clouds. Somehow, we formulate in our mind, what, and who can fill that empty love tank we are carrying. It's imperative to address and fix your own issues before you explore the possibility of marriage. Check out his/her personality, and emotional temperament. Is he or she extroverted or suppressive? Warm or cold? Loud or quiet? Expressive or suppressive? Please don't overlook the quality of being mentally and emotionally healthy.

Another strong value that must be explored is how does he/she manage finances? Does he/she believe in giving? How is his/her credit rating? Is another paycheck needed the day after payday? All these things must be considered before entering into an emotional attachment. Once the attachment is firm and solid, it is extremely difficult to pull away from the relationship.

Question 24

Can you have a positive soul tie between a man and a woman prior to being married? Perhaps, while in a courtship or dating situation?

FH:

Yes, you can have a positive soul tie. The dating process is strictly for discovery, not to develop soul-ties. Once you have developed soul ties, it is difficult to disconnect. Therefore, before you allow a soul-tie to develop, get to really know that person. Once you have "fallen in love," it is difficult to be sufficiently objective, reasonable, and logical. Emotions flutter and reasoning goes out the window: the heart dominates the head. When you are in love, you'll have a tendency to overlook faults, ignore danger signals that are obvious to others, and to dismiss the counsel of mature persons. Take heed to deceptively little things that may pop up from time to time. Use wisdom when choosing a mate. Keep your criteria before you at all times and stick with it.

LH:

Explore the values that he and she share. What are your beliefs about marriage? Does he/she believe that marriage is like a hobby? Is marriage placed on a shelf and removed at your discretion? I am alarmed at the number of men who believe they've been called to the "cummerbund" or polygamy ministry. Sadly, the old HBO TV series, "Big Love" has not helped men in remaining faithful to their wives. The show depicts the Mormon Christianity belief that men can have several wives, including children from these various wives. They are considered one happy family. Few boundaries are established – only the fact, that they live in separate houses.

Question 25

How are we to view loneliness?

LH:

Loneliness means there is something void in you, and there is an expectation that you are not fulfilling in your life.

FH:

You can still be married and be lonely. Loneliness is absent of purpose.

LH:

You are not satisfied with yourself and you're not celebrating yourself, but looking for someone else to validate you. You have to be able to do that for yourself. That's the difference in walking around being confident and waiting for someone for affirmation.

FH:

But also, what you can do is keep your schedule full. Where productive steps are you taking toward your destiny? Not just looking at TV shows, but reading a book, going to an opera or a play? Are you participating in enjoyable activities that will open up your world? You have to expand your perspective and interests. It may be that your world is too limited. Locate people that are smarter than you in your area of interest, and are working in your preferred field. Expand your contacts: go on a trip that is adventurous. Join a small group, take a class. Just do something different this year. You never know where that Mr. Right or Mrs. Right is located. Stop confining them to your small circle of friends and interests.

Question 26

Explain this statement, better to marry than to burn.

FH:

When you look it up the definition, it means to *burn* in the passion of lust. It means that you put yourself through traumatic situations and struggles. When you are a single person and exposed to intimacy to the degree that it provokes your passion, you are allowing a crop to fester. You are creating a fire, it then begins to burn. Eventually, it becomes a raging campfire. So, if you are going to walk this walk as a single person, you have to take mastery, and manage your environment. Take control of your surroundings: you must manage what's entering through your eye gate and ear gate, and especially what's leaving out of your mouth. In other words, you have to manage yourself.

LH:

One thought is meant to lead you to another thought until you've got emotions that are raging, because it becomes like a feeding tube.

Question 27

How long should you know a person prior to marriage?

FH:

I suggest you get to know that person for at least two years. It takes at least that long for you to discover that person.

LH:

Everyone puts their good foot out first: showing their best behavior. But, eventually the real person evolves into their "true self."

FH:

If a person can't control their thought life, they aren't able to control their physical life.

LH:

Our minds are continually "under construction," analyzing new information. Simultaneously, our minds are disarming, dismantling, and capturing other unfruitful, information that attempt to seep its way into our subconscious. Watch out! Harmful information can get a footing and create mass destruction for your life.

Question 28

How do you deal with loss in a relationship?

FH:

One of the major skills we must all master in life is the ability to cope with loss.

LH:

This loss can appear in many forms; loss of a loved one, loss of self-esteem, a role, self-control, financial security, or a fantasy relationship. When we fail to adjust to loss, many find themselves oppressed and depressed. I have experienced a series of losses throughout my life.

FH:

You must have inner strength. Inner strength is inward fortitude, stamina, and persistence. It is the ability to remain calm under pressure. Godly inner strength comes from peace.

LH:

The secret to renewing your strength is WAITING on the Lord. Although you may be hurting, you must "Wait." You're crying, but "WAIT!" You've missed it, but Wait on the Lord, and everything is going to be all right!

Question 29

How do you prevent becoming fooled?

FH:

Don't be duped into believing him or her when their actions are completely contrary to what they are saying. Have you heard the saying, "Your actions speak so loudly, I can't hear what you are saying?" When you remain in this type of relationship, self-doubt starts to surface. He may even try to convince you that you shouldn't believe what you just viewed!

LH:

Don't listen with your emotions, listen with your eyes! If they don't treat friends in ways that you admire, then what makes you think they will treat you better than what you've observed? A strong character indicator of whether they are a potential mate is by looking at their friends. Consider the old axiom, "Birds of a feather flock together."

FH:

Basically, we associate with people who are similar to us in values, attitudes, personality, age, status, and lifestyle! Certain people just aren't good marriage material. They are selfish by nature, and always looking to receive something that they themselves aren't willing to give up. Listen! Don't turn your head toward the red light.

Question 30

Oral sex, is it okay in a marriage?

FH:

That's such a controversial topic in the body of Christ. It is something that needs to be discussed prior to marriage. Oral sex is something that both parties should enjoy. If it's offensive to one, then it must be discussed thoroughly, and possibly not permitted in the relationship. If it's your conviction not to participate in any sexual act that is uncomfortable or against your belief, then it shouldn't be allowed in the marriage bed.

Question 31

Is it ok to live together prior to marriage?

FH:

By all means I would say NO! Many people are cheapening themselves by giving themselves to someone, who hasn't committed to them. Why get entangled into living with someone who doesn't want to commit to you.

LH:

Biblically, it is not spiritually based, and looking at statistics, it's not favorable. Living together before getting married doesn't accomplish the goal that many couples believe. A couple who does not live together prior to getting married has a 20 percent chance of being divorced within 5 years. If the couple has lived together beforehand, that number jumps to 49 percent. At that 10-year mark, a married couple has a 33 percent chance of breaking up. For the unmarried couple who is living together, the likelihood of a breakup is a whopping 62 percent!

Question 32

How do you know when you are ready to explore a relationship?

FH:

Before you are ready to embrace someone else, you first must embrace yourself. Being happy and enjoying your single status is too critical. Many people will place their lives on hold, just waiting in limbo, instead of forging ahead and appreciating the journey. Whatever crack is open in the door of your emotions, it will be identified. You must deal with any discontent. The Word says, "We are complete in Him, perfect and entire, wanting nothing," (see James 1:4, NLT).

LH:

If you are discontent being single, now is not the time to entertain the thought of getting married. I always say, "If you're hungry, any and everything looks good!" You can't be desperate and searching for a mate at the same time. During a time of desperation, you will allow anyone to fill the void. When my husband and I met, I was a hot mess! I was broken in pieces from making seriously wrong relationship choices! Obviously, I was not in any good condition to be looking for a mate. My previous relationships were extremely abusive, to say the least. I was the typical young girl raised by a single mom, who for all intents and purposes, raised her children to the best of her ability. As a result, I transitioned into adulthood ill-equipped, and misinformed on how to make wise decisions. Unfortunately, when my husband and I met, I didn't know how to act.

Question 33

What are your thoughts on Internet dating?

FH:

In today's society, various Internet dating websites promise to find true love mates for men and women.

LH:

Sure, I have heard both positive and negative responses from individuals who have dared to take the risk. Some have found the love of their life, while others were tricked, schemed and defrauded in believing they were getting Mr. or Mrs. Right.

FH:

Unfortunately, they didn't fit the total bill. We have become naïve to the fact that just because it looks good on paper, doesn't mean that in actuality it is a match made under heaven.

LH:

By answering a questionnaire, dating websites promise to locate the perfect man or woman of your dreams. These questionnaires are designed to identify similarities between you and a prospective partner. You soon realize that compatibility involves far more than having things in common. Without the fundamental element of your belief being in common, you are in for a rollercoaster ride through life.

FH:

Complementarily refers to the extent to which differences benefit both partners. Two people are usually drawn together by their similarities and their differences. Who wants a "yes man" or a "yes woman" as a partner to process duplicate thoughts in their minds? Life will start to look boring and all the shades of color will appear the same. Plus, why would you want to marry your own reflection? Before you explore a relationship on the Internet, get to really know the person. You must familiarize yourself with that person, not through a computer, but in person.

FH:

Find his weakness, strengths, and how he responds in difficult situations. Reflect on his personality, values and family background before you go any further. Of course, we all have weaknesses, but think about this: "Can I live with him and what are my deal breakers in a relationship?" If there aren't any boundaries set, then you are sure to be violated in some form or another. Here's the real test: Are you a better person with or without him/her.

Question 34

How do I move on from a married state to healthy single state?

FH:

In order to move on from a marital state to a healthy single state, self-examination is required. You must sort out this unfortunate, horrible time in your life. You need to look back on the marriage to determine what actually went wrong.

LH:

A lesson unlearned is bound to be repeated. You can become a better person if you use what you learned to make changes. As you reflect on your past, I'm sure you'll discover that poor communication has been one of the cohorts in the marriage break-up. Another major element in a marital break-up is getting hitched for the wrong reasons. Innumerable amounts of people enter into marriage with unreasonable expectations.

FH:

If you aren't happy with yourself, no one else can make you happy! Since no one is perfect, you are certain to be hurt, disappointed, and misunderstood. Heartbreak is and will always be part of life – period. Broken trust is often a primary reason for the failure of a marriage. Once trust is broken, it's like glass – almost impossible to put back together. This is especially true if the severity of the broken glass is busted in minuscule pieces.

Question 35

So where do I go from here?

FH:

For those recently divorced or on the brink of divorce, you may wonder, "Where do I go from here?" Well, you must first accept the fact that you are single or soon-to-become single. This is not the end of your life! Your destiny consists of more than being married. It's time to make the most of this fresh start in your life!

LH:

Accept the present and develop your gifts and talents. Constantly repeat affirmations of peace over your life. "And the peace of God, which transcends all understanding, will guard your hearts and your minds in Christ Jesus," (Philippians 4:7).

Question 36

What do you do when you think there isn't anyone for you?

FH:

Tribulation becomes the gateway through which God takes us where He wants us to go. He uses trouble as our ticket to promotion. It's my success and failures that is helping to shape my destiny. Both have worked as a team to develop you.

LH:

You must learn to live with your past, flaws, and circumstances, and to succeed nonetheless. My father was a photographer and I remember many times watching him develop film in the dark room. It was always an arduous process for the film to develop and transform from a slight image to a visual picture. Little by little, you would get a clear perspective of what was "transforming." After various solutions were applied to the film itself, it was then hung to dry, so the final process could be completed. How many times have you felt your life was in developmental stages? Once you thought you had arrived to your life's destination, here comes another hurdle for you to jump. The unexpected challenge left you feeling like you were in a dark place. You weren't able to see a glimpse of light from any direction. Every place you turned for answers or comfort didn't offer any help or reassuring words.

FH:

You may be in a dark place in your life, but we are your "coaches" and we are cheering you on to victory. But, James 1:2 says, "Consider it pure joy, my brothers, whenever you face trails of many kinds, because you know that the testing of your faith develops perseverance.

LH:

Faith is like film it develops in the dark.

Question 37

How do you develop hope in a hopeless situation?

FH:

There is nothing in life that God can't heal! When I divorced it was a difficult thing. I had four kids to raise on my own. But God spoke to me so clearly and said that He was going to use my divorce as a testimony for others. Surely, He has been faithful to His Word. Out of your mess surely comes a message of hope and restoration!

LH:

When I divorced, I never thought in a million years that my life would turn out this way. I never dreamed of having such an incredible life. God has done more than I ever could imagined. My prayer for you is that God, does exceedingly, abundantly more than you could ever imagine. The past is behind, so look beyond the pain, disappointments, and the shattered fairytale dream. There is a new day dawning, right beyond the horizon!

Question 38

So exactly what are the steps to build my future, especially when I'm hurting?

FH:

Ask God to heal you from something that's been bothering you.

LH:

Ask God to reveal to you the past memory that still hurts you.

FH:

Recognize that change happens over time. You must patient with yourself.

LH:

Pray this prayer: "I renounce hatred, anger, resentment, revenge, retaliation, unforgiveness and bitterness in the name of Jesus. I forgive any person who has ever hurt me, disappointed me, abandoned me, mistreated me, or rejected me in the Name of Jesus. I renounce all fear, unbelief, and doubt in the Name of Jesus. I renounce all selfishness, self-will, self-pity, self-rejection, self-hatred and self-promotion in the Name of Jesus. And, I renounce all ungodly thought patterns and belief systems in the Name of Jesus!

Question 39

What are some pointers in being a good mate?

FH:

You must be His Encourager. The male ego can either be demolished by his wife or built up by her. The word "encouragement" means; to give courage, hope or confidence to, give support, be favorable, and foster help.

LH:

My husband always asks me after he has ministered, "How did I do?" No matter what others say to him, what I tell my husband has the most lasting affect. Therefore, I choose to be his best cheerleader, rooting him on, staying attentive while he's ministering and displaying a look of, "I got your back." You can actually empower him to become the best man possible. Recognize what God wants to do in their lives, and water that potential with words of encouragement and affirmation!

FH:

Be sexually open and free. Encouragement and being sexually open and free go hand-in-hand. It's not the plan of God for you not to have good sex.

LH:

Therefore, make it a priority. Discuss it and make it plain and clear, so there is no room for open doors.

FH:

Sex fulfills his male ego by allowing him to demonstrate his role as husband and lover. It definitely reduces friction in the home, and provides one of life's most exciting experiences. It's OK to be "sexy" for your husband. You are the answer for every desire he may possess.

LH:

You must be willing to challenge yourself to grow in areas so that you can fulfill your role as a helpmate. Don't limit yourself to a small existence of knowing how to make spaghetti. Make things happen. This will sharpen him and push him to reach further and expand his horizon as well.

FH:

Take care of your body, through exercise, and eating nutritious meals. I know age accumulates inches, but they don't have to find a resting home in undesirable places. Join a gym; take a walk through the neighborhood.

LH:

Stay disciplined in your spiritual life. The last thing he needs is an emotional, unstable, and unpredictable woman he always has to rescue from anxiety and depression.

FH:

Most men, like all us, want to know what to expect. Maintain consistency and predictability. He shouldn't have to question whom he is returning home to each day.

LH:

Choose to be a happy person; lighten up with life. Everything is not always as it appears. Your husband wants a fun-loving wife to greet him when he comes home from work. He is in a war zone in the world; make his home a place of refuge. He also wants her to take pride in her home and her role as wife and mother.

FH:

Don't allow him to hide his feelings by becoming a workaholic. It turns into a hiding place for his fear of failure. Prevent him from using his work as an excuse not to live more fully in other areas. It also becomes a place of escape for feelings of aggression as well. Build him up daily, he has a HUGE job! Mother his children with love, compassion and tenderness. He's depending on you to secure a home environment of warmth and growth for his children.

Question 40

How do you deal with shame in regards to being in an unhealthy relationship?

LH:

By definition, shame is a deep sense of inferiority. Feelings of inadequacy can destroy your feeling of self-worth. It has been proven that we behave in a manner that is consistent with our perception of ourselves. If you can change your perception of yourself, you can change the behavior. And, if I can change my behavior, I will ultimately change the course of my life. You are not in subjugation to your past: Your past has only been a *temporary* detour to your future.

Occasionally, when driving, I run into a sign that says, "Detour." A detour is only an alternate means to reach my appointed destination. The detour may take me a little out of the way or a bit longer to get back to my final purpose or aim. But, if I follow the detour sign correctly, trust the instructions, and be patient, I will get there.

FH:

When past failures, and dissatisfaction emerges to an all-time high, shame enters. Too often, our self-image rests solely on an evaluation of our past behavior, being measured only through memories. Can you imagine buying stock based on the references of a consumer, who purchased the same stock five years ago? Society has dramatically changed within the last several years. Yet, day-after-day, year-after-year, people build their future and hopes upon the rubble of yesterday's failures.

Much of today's decisions are being based solely on actions of the past. Why? Some haven't pulled their thoughts out of the pasts' pile of garbage. But, we can change!

We can persevere and overcome! You must be released from your old self-concept, which was founded in failure. To accomplish this, you must base your self-worth on God's opinion of you. Trust in His Spirit to bring about change in your life.

Question 41

I feel like my life has been affected by regret, is that possible?

FH:

Regret has a way of pulling and holding you back. It actually causes you to have fear, where you are paralyzed and unable to move. Its counter-part is distraction. The continual lingering memory of the past is a distraction, keeping you from reaching forward. The cousin of regret is bitterness: It loves to bind you to what's possible for your life. Regret always keeps you facing backwards. Unfortunately, living in your historic past will drive you into the cul-de-sac of emotional pain, loss of time, and life.

LH:

Regret starts with a bad experience, that transitions into self-punishment. Here are some things that will help you deal with shame;

Step 1: Renounce mental replays. Erase images associated with the bad memory: They sustain and fuel it. Read 2 Corinthians 10:5.

Step 2: Talk it out. Find someone you can trust. You should have seven people in your life that will encourage you and tell you the truth. Make yourself accountable to them and speak with them regularly. Talking it out has a way of bringing understanding. When you talk about it – the issue no longer holds you captive. When truth is revealed, lies are exposed.

Step 3: Remind yourself that forgiveness is necessary for your freedom. Read 1 John 1:9. Step 4: Put the past behind you. There are no such things as "forgiving and forgetting." Let's face it. Once memories are logged in our mental computer, they are there for life. Thankfully, "forgetting" is not a prerequisite for healing our wounds – nor is it necessary for forgiveness. What is necessary is that we face the facts of our wounds, relinquish replays, and revenge.

Question 42

When do I know it's time to try love again?

FH:

A few questions you may want to ponder upon before entering a relationship: Am I ready to trust again? Am I complete, and fulfilled in my state of singleness? Or, am I looking for someone to complete me? And, am I emotionally stable to give a relationship 100 percent?

LH:

My husband and I were recently counseling a young man who was betrayed by his wife. He consciously decided that love costs too much. So, he shut up his heart, making a subconscious decision to never love again or be vulnerable with any woman. His heart became hardened because of the buried sorrow. Fortunately, this young man is now in the healing process. For many, the pain can be so intense, that you are in denial. When the pain is still present, that could possibly be an indicator that it is not quite time to love again.

Question 43

What are the steps to build my future, especially when I'm hurting?

FH:

There are a few steps that I recommend taking:

(1.) Ask God to heal you from something that's been bothering you.

(2.) Ask God to remove the pain of those memories and heal you.

(3.) Recognize that change takes place over time.

(4.) You know you are healed when you do not hide memories, but can share them freely.

LH:

Say this prayer: I renounce hatred, anger, resentment, revenge, retaliation, unforgiveness and bitterness. I forgive any person who has ever hurt me, disappointed me, abandoned me, mistreated me or rejected me. I renounce all fear, unbelief, self-will, self-pity, self-rejection, and self-hatred. And, I renounce all ungodly thought patterns and belief systems in the name of Jesus!

FH:

I need you to know that God is sifting carefully through the sawdust and scrap piles of old ruins in your life. God is repairing you right now!

Question 44

I literally hate being single, what should I do?

FH:

The Oxford Dictionary defines the word monument as; a marker, shrine, gravestone or tomb. We have erected large, invisible, high-risers in our minds that have apparently become insurmountable monuments of destruction. Sometimes, we can easily want something so badly that we have erected it as a monument in our lives.

LH:

We place people and relationships as monuments in our lives. Despite how we are treated, we refuse to remove the monuments from their fixed positions in our hearts and minds. Thus, we have become co-dependent on unhealthy relationships. Ultimately, the monuments become humongous, and what began as simple coping mechanisms or need, take on lives of their own. We are on a merry-go-round, and we can't jump off!

FH:

Begin to ask yourself, "Exactly, where is my desperation coming from? What false belief have I established in my mind? Am I living my life to the fullest? And, exactly what am I requiring in a mate? Until that person comes along, take this time to prepare yourself for when he/she comes into your life.

Question 45

So, I want to be married, what is the next step?

LH:

Marriage is a great under-taking, full of life-altering decisions, sacrifice, and a whole lot of unselfishness. But, on the other hand, it is rewarding, exciting and very fulfilling. The first step, is to write down the description of how the ideal male or female appears to you. Separate your list into the following components; spiritually, emotionally, socially, economically, physically, and mentally. Under each heading, compile at least seven expectations according to the most important to the least. Also, make a list of qualities or attributes that are necessary in your life for them to possess. Afterwards, make a list of deal-breakers in the relationship. This is your first-step and acts as a gauge in choosing a mate.

FH:

From this same list write down descriptions of what your ideal self would appear vs. your actual present appearance. Compare your expected list of them to your list. This acts as your own barometer in inspecting your own life. What you expect from others, you need to exemplify in your life. Allow the Holy Spirit to start or continue His transformation process in your life. Let His surgical instruments gently begin to cut away layers of your unhealthy self. He will snip away the roots that have become firmly intertwined with every facet of your life. You can't expect someone to bring something to the table, you yourself can't produce.

Question 46

I'm really going to dig deep into preparing for marriage, where do I begin?

FH:

Since you want to dig deep, let's begin. Here are some things you may want to consider. Write three things that you like most about yourself, and three things you like least. Afterwards, complete this sentence: My greatest personal strength is (fill-in the blank), and my greatest personal weakness is (fill-in the blank).

LH:

Here are some additional soul-searching things to consider. When I'm afraid, I usually respond by (fill in the blank) and how I would like to respond is (fill-in the blank). When I'm sad, I usually respond by (fill-in the blank). How I'd like to respond (fill-in the blank). And when I'm angry, I usually respond by (fill-in the blank), and How I'd like to respond (fill-in the blank).

In general, I think most men are (fill-in the blank). In general, I think most women are (fill-in the blank). And finally, what I fear most is (fill-in the blank), and what I need most is (fill-in the blank).

You are ready now to begin your journey of discovery.

Question 47

Is it OK not to have a desire to be married?

FH:

Absolutely! It is fine not to have a desire to be married. There are those who desire not to have children as well. When it comes to making a permanent life-altering decision, it must be thoroughly examined and explored. The worst thing you can do is make a permanent decision, based on a temporary desire or need.

LH:

I totally agree. You don't marry because it's the norm. What's someone else's normalcy doesn't have to be yours. When you face the truth that being married is not your desire, you are free to pursue your life single to the fullest. When your heart decides a destination, your mind will design a map to reach it.

Question 48

I desire to be married, but I feel extremely unstable at times. Can you help me?

FH:

Through our thoughts and our words, we often dig holes for ourselves. A hole is where there is no forward progression, no forward motion. You are trapped and sometimes buried in the hole you dug for yourself. So how do you get out of the hole? Stop digging - the more you dig, the deeper the hole, and the harder it is to get out. And then you must look up. Looking down has no value and has not helped your situation. Finally, you need to ask for help from someone who is not in the hole with you.

LH:

Ask yourself the following "Test of Character" questions.

1). What type of man or woman, in your estimation, is marriage material? 2). How do you judge their character? 3). What do they add to your life? 4). Are they an asset or liability? Why?

Finally, "What are your resume" questions; 1). What attributes do you have to offer? 2). Are you an asset or a liability? And if so, why?

Question 49

Can certain infractions that happened to me as a young child inhabit my relationships now that I'm an adult?

FH:

Yes, there are fractures in your early foundations, caused either by wounds inflicted upon you, or by responses to events in your life. We are often broken by those events, and it weakens our ability to stand in the time of trial or in the face of a crisis. I want you to know that because you are born anew in Jesus, you are in the position to start over! Your foundation is rebuilt upon the Rock who is Jesus!

LH:

As previously mentioned in question 27: Our minds are continually "under under construction," and constantly retrieving, sorting, filtering and analyzing new information, Simultaneously, our minds are disarming, dismantling and capturing other unfruitful information that attempts to seep its way into our subconscious. Watch out! Harmful information can get a footing and create mass destruction for your life. If I can't control my thought life, I'm unable to control my physical life.

Today is the day to stop accepting your present, temporary situation as your future, permanent situation. Despite your current circumstances, make up your mind to get on with your life. Today is the day to walk by faith - right out of your present circumstances!

Question 50

Before I get engaged what are some of the questions to ask myself?

LH:

My foremost question would be, "what do I expect"? Perhaps no other question is so critical to the success of your relationship. When you think about it, there is nothing more debilitating than overpromising and under delivering. Many enter a relationship with expectations that one or both parties can't fulfill.

FH:

Another question to ask oneself is what are my most prized possessions? Because a person's most valuable possession provides a window into their priorities. Will your individual pursuits converge into shared interests or pull apart with competing agendas? This is so important because many married couples spend their lives competing against each other instead of completing each other.

LH:

What are the roles of a husband and a wife for you? This question gets back to the nature of individual expectations. Some are of the belief of the traditional role, where the male is the breadwinner and the female is the homemaker. Others have a more contemporary view of roles with both spouses working outside the home. Whereas, a progressive view includes a stay at home dad raising the kids while the mom provides income through her career.

FH:

How do you handle disagreements and disappointments? Consider your cooling off period, will it be 24 hours before continuing the conversation? Or perhaps involve your parents, his parents, an ex-boy or girl friend? You would be surprised how people choose to settle disputes outside of the relationship. And consider what is your panic button and how will your partner know when it is sounded? Will dishes be thrown across the room, or a sudden clap appeared across their face? Honesty must be expressed so the other person has a full view of what life will be with you.

LH:

Let's discuss normalcy. Each of us brings a different idea of normalcy into our relationship. We bring baggage into our relationships, whether we are conscious of it or not. Our personal histories, experiences, and personalities carry a combined weight that influences every area of our lives. We generally have different traditions and conflicting ideas.

FH:

Do you forgive easily? Grudge spread through a marriage or relationship like cancer invades our healthy cells, attacking organs at a rapid speed. If you lose your willingness to change, you have lost your willingness to survive. This includes humility and ability to admit our mistakes and ask for forgiveness. Before you marry, create in yourself an openness to change and an understanding that much correction will be needed for what you will face together. Believe it or not, it is easier to jump off the boat than it is to get back on. And then you must be careful that in claiming your space you don't fool around and show your spouse how to live with you. Sometimes, what we perceive as a need for space is really a need for respect, for direct communication, both asking and receiving, and for change.

Question 51

I grew up without my father. What should I expect my husband to give our daughter?

FH:

Women who grow up without fathers often struggle with feelings of low self-esteem and unworthiness.

LH:

He should teach your daughter how to be in a nonsexual, intimate relationship with a man. He should be the example of unconditional love, honor and being a role model of how a man should treat her. He should be the standard for your daughter in choosing a mate.

FH:

Fatherless girls are more likely to drop out of school, suffer from depression or other emotional disorders and mask their pain through increased promiscuity. Fathers are a mirror to their daughters, reflecting a girl's self esteem back on her. Girls raised with their fathers know that their worth comes from what is between their ears, not what's between their legs.

Question 52

I know I need to begin taking responsibility for my life before entering into another relationship, how do I begin the process?

FH:

Taking stewardship over your life means learning to admit when your problems are the results of your irresponsibility rather than finding excuses. People who "own" their problems tend to mature much faster than those who excuse or transfer blame.

LH:

Learn to respect others' differences. One indication of a selfish person is an inability to live with another person.

FH:

Taking responsibility is so very important. Willingness to take responsibility for your own life is critical. Assuming responsibility for oneself isn't easy in this modern world. We have been conditioned all our lives to blame every external circumstance and every other person around us for the parts of our lives we don't like. You must become a participant in your own rescue by taking ownership of your own destiny. The biggest demon for most people is their own unwillingness to realistically confront themselves and their future. Your future is controlled by you and you alone, regardless of the shifting winds of change that are blowing all around you.

LH:

If you want things to get better in your life, you have to get better. If you want things to change, you have to change. If you want things to improve or grow or increase, you have to improve or grow or increase.

FH:

When you step up to the plate and accept responsibility for your own decisions and for the circumstances you have created in the past and create in the future, you will feel more positive about yourself and happier with life. You will feel like you are finally guiding your own ship and controlling your own destiny. You can realize all the great potential that your Creator has placed within you if you will take responsibility for yourself and then do what's necessary to turn things around. Let's get busy. Let's reveal the proven things you can do to improve those areas of your life.

About the Authors

Fred and Linda Hodge are Pastors of Living Praise Christian Center in both Chatsworth and Palmdale, California. Through their 34 years of marriage and ministry experience they have developed tremendous knowledge and insight in cultivating people for success in life. Although Fred and Linda experienced divorce in their past, they choose to become better not bitter and mastered the art of choosing wisely. A principle they share with audiences throughout their travels.

They are known for their practical approach to life and through their transforming messages provoke both singles and marrieds to live in their best "state" for the present while intentionally moving forward into their future endeavors. Together they have authored 5 books, traveled throughout the United States, equipping people for "next level" living.

Known to many as the "power couple," Fred and Linda live by the conviction that quality of life can be achieved by all who are willing to push beyond their limiting beliefs and experience the breakthrough of transformation teaching. The results of Fred & Linda's mentoring and coaching throughout the years has caused many to acquire a fulfilled life and yield fruits that produced abundant life.

www.ingramcontent.com/pod-product-compliance
Lightning Source LLC
Chambersburg PA
CBHW070552300426
44113CB00011B/1880